Propaganda

By the same author

Knowing and Forgetting

Propaganda

Michael Hulse

Secker & Warburg
London

First published in England 1985 by
Martin Secker & Warburg Limited
54 Poland Street, London W1V 3DF

Copyright © Michael Hulse 1985

British Library Cataloguing in Publication Data

Hulse, Michael
    Propaganda.
    I. Title
    821'.914   PR6058.U39/

    ISBN 0-436-20966-7

Printed in Great Britain by
Redwood Burn Limited
Trowbridge, Wiltshire.

to the memory of my mother
and for my father

Acknowledgements

Most of these poems were previously printed or broadcast in *Ambit, Aquarius, Argo, BBC Radio 3 'Poetry Now', Critical Quarterly, Encounter, Kudos, Literary Review, London Magazine, New Edinburgh Review, Outposts, Poetry Durham, Straight Lines* and the *Times Literary Supplement;* in Australia in *Helix, Poetry Australia* and *Quadrant,* and in Canada in *Antigonish Review.* An ealier version of 'The Whale' was written for the Canadian anthology *Whales: A Celebration,* edited by Greg Gatenby. Many of the poems appear here in revised form.

. . . *the test of a first-rate intelligence is the ability to hold two opposed ideas in the mind at the same time, and still retain the ability to function.*

F. Scott Fitzgerald

Doublethink means the power of holding contradictory beliefs in one's mind simultaneously, and accepting both of them.

George Orwell

Contents

III

I

*There can be no such thing as a life
that wasn't meant for the person who has it.*

Louis Simpson

Windowless Monads

See how the houses crowd about
the skirts of the hennish church like chickens:
so cosy and close to God,

the comfortable homes of happy families.
Firewood is tidily stacked in the dry;
the axe lies in the dust, a shine

blazing from the blade. Being
may be a bright coincidence; our words
are not the language of things; our smiles

are smiles we have learnt from photographs.
Put up your hair, my love. The nape of your neck
is the home of closeness to me. See

how waiters run to the woman in fox and gauze,
see how the coffee steams, how the cream is white,
see the labour of cake that man has created.

These things must give us pause. Even
a pavement café can tell us about our lives;
even a coffee cup includes our love.

Put up your hair and join me, come
and join me out on our balcony of time.
The sun has turned to thunder: but do not

be afraid, it has always been like this,
the waiters watching the coffee cups fill with rain,
the cake disintegrating gracefully.

The Whale

Poised for the
leap, the pole-vaulter
pulses with his

future. The potter
pressures time
into form. The actor

creates dimensions
to move in.
Revolutionaries:

all of them, all
the seagreen incorruptibles,
the makers of transformation,

working to wrest from the stasis of time
the cardiac apprehension of beauty,
the sudden arrest of perception.

And somewhere the blue-backed past
breaks the black salt, the cold
confidence of the dream

we had harboured deep in warmth,
and shows us sculpture and stone
unsundered, living, in motion.

Tangle

Led on and then abandoned by a
blindness: taking the trains and travelling
light, trusting wire with words

that carry my luggage of love, and ending
the dull unsimple anomie here
in the quiet dark of the city of Mark,

knowing that all my life is in
this anoetic ravelling in the heart,
this harder beat in the throat: no,

you are right, of course, of course you are right,
there must be more to us than love. Although
I like my life enough to want to love you.

Across the shining black lagoon
acataleptic vaporettos ply
like thoughts across the surface of the mind,

exempla of a true hypothesis
I do not even care to try to prove.
I am happiest knowing I cannot know,

breathing the deep sea tang and beating
back the tears and brushing the hair from your face,
not even caring I cannot prove my love:

the rest is canals and the nasty madness
of passages and alleyways and night,
the abject tangle of an Aschenbach.

Loreley

Ich weiß nicht, was soll es bedeuten,
daß ich so traurig bin . . . though who could sit
by the cold river, watching the lights

of the opposite bank, St Goarshausen,
shake in the ferry's wake, then settle again
to a steady glow of gold

molten on the flow (und ruhig
fließt der Rhein), and not
know that this is the off-season

of love . . .? Ein Märchen aus alten Zeiten,
das kommt mir nicht aus dem Sinn: in
the corner the cook is drinking himself silly,

telling the boss and the barman for
the third time this evening the story about
the Danzig whore. Presently they sing.

They seem to have made no preparations for winter,
but nothing will stop their noise, not even the silence,
not even the autumn's big and childless voids.

Egon Schiele Considers the Sunflower

I,
the autumn onanism of
a summer love of colour,

a sulphur smoulder of gold,
the brown of turned earth,
dirty green.

What dullness wears this drab
habit? I
will paint myself, myself

coming fully to a sum,
brittle as a withered stick,
desire abiding the fire.

Guided Tour, Orphic

The Janus moment: pushing forward
into our own foreknown conclusions, we yet
yearn to look back.

Entrances and exits:
our own lives
inching out the infinite line.

We listen, see little, and form
patterns in the rooms, like soldiers
squared but then broken, randomly.

The walls are woven over with myths.
This man is paid to explain
the mysteries we are living in.

Soon to be a Major Film

The best stories begin with sirens whining,
the traffic pulling in to the side and waiting
for fear to go flashing by. The black-clad biker lying

dying in a pool of public blood
was on his way to Lisa, who at this moment
is serving a sundae with a Bunny dip

in an ice-salon on the wrong side of town. The story's
as much about her father, though, who made
his packet selling indulgences and retired

at forty-five to a villa near Trieste
where he'd throw parties for papal nuncios keen
on keeping up their CIA connections.

The mixture as before. The rights
to this poem have been sold to MGM.
Cut to an autumn afternoon in Poland,

the copper-colour wasting into grey,
lyrical tones: a passionate young Catholic
enthusiastically fondles the word freedom

and priggishly complains that in the West
there are fashions even in seriousness.
I really ought to write more of this narrative stuff.

Welcome to the Delectable Mountains

The shadows of our doubts
darken the grass and treetops as we rise.
Here we are at the beginning and end

of all natural scenery, paying our way
up the mountainside: they are taking us
for a ride. The cable car

translates us cautiously to a glacial
pinnacle of inwardness
where Alps on Alps arise

and hang-gliders are stepping off
the cliff-face of Error, purposefully
throwing themselves into nothing.

Look, here you can work a telescope with a coin,
make low the hills and mountains and exalt
the valleys. The closer the landscape comes

the more the grey of distance is upon it:
who will say that seeing is believing?
A girl says it's nothing in summer,

you should be here in the season.
She speaks of snow-capped peaks
and strange exhilarations on the piste,

the singing of air in her ears
and the swift vigour of the down down down
of wishes fulfilled: innocence

perfected in perception of its limits.
She doesn't say quite this;
I am interpreting.

I say it must be quite something,
and she looks at me as if to say
she can see I don't really understand.

In fact I am thinking of a trip
from Hanley High, when I was in the first form:
a fat boy, and the climb up Snowdon was

hot bloody slog, but sliding down the side
could satisfy a boy's imagination.
Excitement and control in one,

sheer energy, the disciplined sense
of descending over the edge of the present tense —
the secret seemed to lie in thinking fast,

thinking past the steps I ought to need:
running down a steep scree,
saving myself with speed.

At Thaxted

All of them, all of them
are walking to the mill
along the stony path

between
the knowing openness
where combed rows of green

grow to a slow
summerness
of fullness.

It is wonderfully good
to be here and to *see*
this field full of folk.

The Kiss

Like mother and daughter folding sheets
the lovers in the elsewhere street
meet, incline and kiss:

the illusory vase
in puzzle books. Nothing exists
but the simple touch of lips,

though maybe their eyes communicate
an acquiescence in the wit
of instinct's sweet cognition,

the imperceptible bodying a presence,
like air around a statue:
love defining its own serenity.

Auguries of Experience

I

The ache of conscience:
the act of contrition wears away
to a war of attrition,

and war itself is worn away
to a sophisticated game
the inheriting meek are forced to play —

these Manichaean checks and balances,
the pros and cons, a matter of life and death
to constitutional lawyers.

They'll have us thinking double. Pros
down to the last discretion and clever con,
briefed on the binding clauses in

our secular contracts, they know all about
the double meanings in our sacred words.
I have seen the munitions manufacturers

playing a quick nine holes before the important meeting,
sociably drinking away the ache:
they cannot think in terms of individuals.

II

Across the road a church is being built.
The scaffolding frame
defines creation as a game:

a cat's cradle of crosspiece and stilt,
Cleopatra's snake and Jacob's ladder,
I'm the king of the castle.

The rules remain the same:
build, build, build — for only construction
can be construed as true propitiation.

The rest is Machiavellian sacrifice,
guilt gone to the guillotine, life to the knife,
mystery written into history:

The Dirty Years' War.
The Age of Treason.
Scaffolding becomes the scaffold.

III

Yet all experience is an arch wherethro'
gleams that untravell'd world, whose margin fades
forever and forever when the foreman,

walking home in the serious light
when unambiguous evening
erases the day in a gradual fading

of nothing nothing night,
finds a child
abandoned

on the infertile lap of ground
that was to be the threshold.
Dead as soon as it was born, they said:

checks and balances and plastic bags,
a birth of innocence and guilt,
propitiation by another name.

One step broken, the great scale's destroy'd:
down the snake, up the ladder,
into the void.

And the war goes on, the diurnal revolution,
the game the flesh is heir to:
this turning dirt, this blue

bundle of cluttered cloud,
this love child of brutality
and hope.

December Evensong

The bookseller locks up his shop
and whistles his bicycle into the slush.
Radetzkies into the Sisley mist.

Freely contracted to a generous bondage
we make our way to church,
aware that our feet and hearts are too cold.

The butcher unhooks his last rabbit.
Our watch-with-mother greetings smile
from face to face and fade.

The moon is a dull Victoria sixpence.
Kicking up the snow,
carol-singers jingle tins from house to house.

The Fountain

The fountain's avowal of sunlight:
the naked water erupted
effortless into the air,

stopped, unsupported,
poised at the apogee,
shot through with sun,

then plummeted into the pool. We too
infallibly renew
our sense of self and soul

through birth and death, the apsides
of our existence. We become
our own continuum.

Balloons

A man is selling balloons from a fistful:
childhood raised a few powers
to a pleasure full of zeros.

Like memory straining into forgetting
they pull, tugging upward. Tension
taut in the need to hold on.

The archivist who bought just one
releases it deliberately. Up
it topples, jostling, up,

bobbing like a bubble in a bottle.
The old man watching from the top floor
follows it up, closes the window, turns away.

The Poplar Field

I remember my grandmother telling me
of Victorian funerals: mortality
bobbing and clopping across the cobbles

behind the horses black as coffins, and from
the horses' foreheads, like fountains, black plumes
topple-topping the procession of loss

like poplars tossed in the wind.
Perishing pleasures . . . The poplars, like pages
riffled in a reference section, repeat

the whispering grief of Cowper's colonnade,
and the leaves lay shade on the restful field,
evening's grey farewell to a greater age.

The Future that Mends Everything

I

Out west a scarlet light
inviting us to whorish night
bloodies the black sky and scatters

the last stars at the corners of aquamarine.
A woman is waiting in the room. Her hair
is turned back from her face like a counterpane.

Her face is naked as a bed. Her eyes
are deep, as if she were asleep, and dreaming.
I do not know why I am here,

listening to the diligent crickets
whittle the night away, wondering
why the lies I believe in aren't the truth.

Now. Do you hear them? singing again, singing,
innocents at knowing Compiègne,
human voices in a forest of symbols,

like children in a fairy tale
frightened at nightfall. Often
I've heard them, singing again, but here

I have remained, repeating my contrition,
the light at the back of my mind a candle
cradled in a wicker, swinging in the wind . . .

I remember after the downpour the vapour
hazily steaming up from the forest
like effort from a horse's flank,

and I was walking beside a field of oats
along the familiar emblematic track
rucked with tractor ruts. It looked

the usual forest, the great grimm forest,
the dark foreboding home of all
my gothic dreams of evil,

and, yes, the shooting blinds were like
watch-towers at Buchenwald, and I
no more than a mover in an allegory.

II

What need have we of allegory, love?
It is the fact that fascinates, the form,
imagination fastening on the laws

of silence, thought impossibly locked
in logic simple as a leaf.
The requiem identifies the dying:

our only subject, mutability
as emblem of mortality, becomes
the birth and death of my only hero, myself . . .

Then I was in the cathedral shade,
where runnelled water rushed like thoughts
through urgencies of undergrowth.

I saw him standing in a clearing
where bracken and bramble grew: a deer,
simple, licit-eyed, each horn

nice as a finely-pointed argument,
perfectly turned, exquisite in intent.
His modest pride reproved

the posing nature of my own
notions of nobility, my poems,
the very forms my knowing takes, will take,

and in the moment of seeing what I loved
I made it an idea of itself; and even now
I cannot write it honestly. I moved,

briefly: but the deer broke and bolted,
was gone almost before I was aware
I'd scared the creature, leaving me

imagining the unsettling scent
of consecration in the air,
innocence in my sights and lost again.

III

This happened as I describe it: cause and effect
as clear as the cry of a child in the dark.
My fictions are far from supreme. But I try.

And now it is dark in the garden here, and I
must think of the pylons policing the naked fields
as I walked back across the acres of guilt

to a home, a community that knows no
end but in the smoke from smouldering leaves
and houses sleeping between the trees.

I must struggle back into childhood, as if
childhood were interrupted sleep
and sleep a desirable dream. I see

them all in a summer night, all,
transfigured by supernal clarity,
like Munch's woman in the wood:

my father, my mother, a family
of smiles and white shirts and summer skirts,
posing for photographs into eternity.

Under a white ciborium of cloud
they stand, celebrants on an altar:
a whole Greek chorus of humanity!

I love them all; and they love me,
loving as Brunelleschi loved the air
he had to crown. I would like to pull down

the terrible dark cathedral, the black
supremities, the meaningless contrition,
and meet the endless opening-out head-on.

A confrontation with the innocence
that we imagine is infinity:
Dreadful, Madam? Fontenelle replied,

I think it pleasant. When the heavens were
a little blue arch, stuck with stars, I found
the universe confined and close, was almost

stifled for want of air; but now it is enlarged
in height and breadth, with a thousand vortexes,
I begin to breathe more freely than before.

The Prisoner

after Rilke

Suppose that what to you is wind and sky,
air that you breathe
and brightness to your eye,

abruptly turns to hurt,
all but that proper part
where your hands are, and your heart;

and what is *tomorrow* to you now,
or *later, then, next year, forever,*
the future sense of promises and hope,

becomes a present tense of pain,
a festering impurity
filling up with suffering;

everything that was you
is nothing but a rawness and a wrong;
and he who once you thought was God

is your gaoler, spiteful, pausing outside
your cell to give you filthy looks.
And still you live.

Rhine Journey in March

Dutch barges surge counter-current,
pushing into the purgative rush.
February's flood receding fast.

The vineyard ribbing
herringbones, like an aerial shot
of Clapham Junction's jostling geometry.

Castles, monotint in grey,
like faded cherries on faded sundaes,
race away in the haze. The train

tunnels and tumbles to Frankfurt,
frantic as a ferret in a hole, faithful to
its categorical imperative.

Deutschland, Deutschland

I

Sunday, soundless and sultry,
an aching, rainless day, ending
in dry thunder: all afternoon

Herr Gutenberg, pretending to read
Mephisto, watches alternately
the silent silver climb the sky

from the American base nearby
and Benno and Bianca playing
tennis with the haphazard happiness

of a beginner and a professional
practising to prove each other in love.
Herr Gutenberg couldn't be better pleased,

and as September assembles the evening
into a gentleness, as if
a hurried darkening would hurt the world,

he takes his walk to the orchard by the river,
a shelving ledge of land where parlour browns
and apple reds blend in the pasture green.

The snail is wrapped asleep on a stalk of parsley.
Bullrushes like distaffs stand stiff
in the dark tranquillity of the water's edge,

a scarlet skiff drifts at its mooring,
and swallows are flying fast and loose
across the earnest surface of the past.

The present has already known the future:
and suddenly he is surprised to find himself
humming *O Haupt voll Blut und Wunden*

and thinking of the room where his mother
died. Death as a science:
drapes dark as morello cherries,

chairs plush with velvet blood,
heavy plum counterpanes and carpets.
Morphallactic silence

in the still, steady air's replete repose:
the shapes of mortality, ready to drop,
dumb with the animal fall,

the soft magic of sudden becoming.
His father kept that room for many years
exactly as she left it at her death,

and used to stand at the window with his son
examining his conscience. For he knew
he hadn't loved her as he might have done.

A wagtail waiting for nothing on a rowlock:
acceptance is everything, and peace
means to accept without a history.

II

In the cathedral square the swingboats bowl
up, and under, sudden, and up again,
thrusting wonder upon the soul.

The fair has come to town. The miracle men
have built their mystical halls of light and sound,
and fantasy, rough beast of bedtime,

is born again; the posters pinned
on fences and on trees proclaim the fact
in colours heraldic as a cigarette packet's,

it must be true. And they have come,
the lovers, the mothers and fathers, the children and dreamers,
determined to love deceit's reality,

while bells above belabour the secular air
with the sacred amazement of elsewhere,
and out the first floor window above

the Einhorn Apotheke an elderly Jew
(who local legend says is a distant
descendant of Mendelssohn who bribed

his way through the War) leans happily out
to see these pleasures innocent of purpose.
All trades conduce to love's success:

a wheel of cheese is V'd at five to ten,
a woman sells a swab of candy floss,
and Benno shoots at thin iconic men

who die with an ironic ping. Bianca
wins a plastic rose for knocking
tins off a shelf, and when she threads it

through her teeth and dances a flamenco
Benno barks a laugh and tells her he loves her
very much. Which Bianca had rather assumed.

Meanwhile the moon investigates
the Moltkestrasse and the Judengasse
and prowls along the Theodor-Heuss-Allee

and even in the darkest happiness
see now, the scythe of birth
shines on the earth.

III

The box that smells of rotting peaches binds
the cemetery in the geometry
of taste: Catholic Germany

clumsily southern, Mediterranean
even in death. He splashes the sign of the cross
with a sprig of box across his parents' grave

and thinks of the wealthy frenchified flesh
that strolled with parasols, whose menfolk built
the villas of the Jugendstil . . . youth

elaborated as an elegance
available to Wilhelmine resources,
a middleness of money, love and truth,

fantasy sternly disciplined to fit
a spirit of perpetual negation
crap-shooting through creation.

He walks with a strident anger he does not
understand to the darkened garden, where
he finds a tennis ball in the grass.

On the verandah, Benno and Bianca
would like to tell him that they plan to marry,
but seeing him fling the ball into the trees

and run inside in wrathful aimlessness
decide it wouldn't be the moment:
he'd only misunderstand.

IV

after Goethe

Peace in the peaks, and in
the pine and poplar tops
the breath of breezes stops:

the birds in the forest have fallen
silent. Soon you too will rest.
Patience.

II

. . . the great thing to learn in this life is to be content with appearances, and shun the vulgarities of the grocer and philosopher.

Katherine Mansfield

A Family Portrait circa 1900

Going blackly back to the old unknown
looking like this! Father, frowning
the future out of countenance;

his beautiful wife wearing a greedy smile
that is smugly defiant, as if she had been caught
secretly nursing proprietary guilt.

Can she suppose nobody knows?
Her eyes are ablaze with praise to the Lord
the Almighty; but she looks bored.

She rests a white hand on the cold shoulder
of the unconsoled girl sitting in front.
Her daughter. Hers for life.

Phrenology, 1914

The music room is cool and blue.
The Essen engineer, her father's friend,
holds the white china head in his broad hands

and examines the cold bald spaces which
a Staffordshire manufacturer has inscribed:
sublimity, benevolence, philoprogenitiveness.

Fräulein Evi finishes, and lays the flute aside.
Bumps on the head, he informs her, smiling,
were said to indicate the size of the brain.

Amazing what people will believe.
Again the supercilious smile
of a man who is on smiling terms with the future.

She knows he has travelled: Morocco, Mexico . . .
She knows the clubmen call him a man of the world.
Her father supposes she will learn to like him.

She knows he holds her father in contempt
for his beliefs, for unfastening his braces after dinner,
for smoking a strong Havana with his cognac.

I think there is a crack across my skull.
He joins her at the window. *It
will open wide if he touches me.*

Magnolia's candescent pallor
cups to candle-flames in the deep green:
waxy ephemera, epigrams of the spirit.

I love you, Evi. And
from far in villa gardens where
the Wannsee air stirs the stillness

and all the August afternoon
innumerable murmurings of bees
negotiate their treaties in the shade

of heavy scented lindens,
an empire's dead imperatives
command immediate consent.

I walked in a poppy field at Potsdam.
Flags of scarlet hanging loose
like rags of slashed flesh.

I put my lips to the petals
and kissed the taste of forgetting.
Who can know what is happening in my head?

When they said we were at war
my mouth went dry with the bleached
taste of the host, like a wafer of wax.

But he is too old to fight and be killed.
I think it may be good to love the dead.
I think I shall scream if he touches me again.

Striking his thigh with a silver-headed cane,
her father crosses the lawn, smiling
to see the engineer stroking her hair.

He is explaining to Reinwald the lawyer
that this our city, our Berlin,
is the nerve centre of the Reich:

all of us must do what we know to be right,
for here we are most sensitive to hurt.
Once more and I shall scream. I wish I could die.

One day I walked out on the Wannsee shore
where Henriette Vogel went with Kleist.
After he had shot her through the heart

he shot himself in the mouth with a second pistol,
and suffocated on the choking smoke
of the powder. Their smiles are smothering me.

The Definition of Surrealism

Six stick insects sitting drinking tea,
spinsters in a wilderness
of witless Chippendale.

This is the meaning of civilization:
six smiling misses in chintzy shifts
lifting brimming cups to thin lips.

English Christian women,
living a birthless sisterhood,
thinking of quintessential sinlessness.

But in from the blonde and blue-eyed past
bursts a battalion of babies, raging
for copulation, threatening rape or gas.

Crisis, Post-prandial

The clock taps like a woman
high-heeling it down a tiled aisle.
Moments spread slowly, raindrops in a pool.

Riffling through *Time*. Finding things to do.
Changing a bulb. The filament jingle:
Appalachian spring.

Appalling after-dinner stupor
of Valpolicella. Spaghetti clogs
the sink like an angler's bait.

Ten past eight . . . Time's
binary fracture, the arms of the clock
like a Stuka diving to strike.

Boredom

This winter the ice
tightens the lake
six inches thick.

You walk across the water
waving to me like
a woman lost awake

from a dream in a lonely hotel.
How I love you! I'd write a poem about it
but the very thought of it leaves me cold.

Fein Liebchen gute Nacht

Byron in Cologne made careful note:
eleven thousand maidenheads of bone,
the greatest number flesh hath ever known.

My saint was St Ursula Andress
anadyomene in *Dr No:*
beyond the virginity principle.

We whisper to a finish, and you lie
like Boucher's Mlle Louise O'Murphy
breast to pillow on the divan, your arse

downy and tender as an apricot;
O the seven seeds of the pomegranate,
the simple spilling, the pleasure.

All the perfect pussies: Kore,
silky Silvia Kristel, sulky Bardot,
and what the Beatles didn't sing,

happiness is a warm cunt. Kore, Kore,
I love you, I'd like to grow old with you,
though for that I can wait. Meanwhile the owl

Ascalaphus is calling, calling, calling you,
loud in the glade. Here's looking at you, kid,
and winter in the underworld.

Kiki Zanzibar

for the girls of the Crazy Horse Saloon, Paris

Kiki trims her triangle and blacks
her pubic geometry to fit
the image of the pack.

Kiki is perfect. All of them are perfect.
Relaxing, sitting straddled on the steps
like dancers in a Degas pastel,

absently
they stroke the hair between their thighs
and smoke and talk unsmilingly.

Kiki pinks her nipples and adjusts
her skullcap, eats a candied peach,
and breathes on the mirror to make believe

she needn't see, slipping a shawl across
her naked shoulders. Strange, to be
a cog in such grotesque machinery.

The boss himself, in Copenhagen,
two years ago, when she was seventeen,
spotted her in a strip-joint, asked her name.

He paid her flight. He liked her style.
She made the grade. She signed the contract.
That was that.

The regiment of flesh:
black leather straps and scarlet stockings,
shiny black boots like a Nazi commandant's.

The martial law of maxi-mouchi-mouchi:
limber limbs simulating
sappy hyped-up happy highs,

and flabby businessmen sweating, calling
oh quel cul tu as, thinking they're cracking
a classy, cosmopolitan joke.

Kiki is sick of it all: the ethic
of nakedness, the discipline
of stimulation, keeping time and smiling.

Now under the tender caresses of the lights
she stretches and flexes and sighs,
satisfied desire desiring more:

like Marion deserted by
her lover in the morning
in the painting by Gervex,

she languishes across
a billowy bed in blissful abandonment:
woman should not be but represent.

Between her thighs the cosmos comes and goes,
communion existing in conception:
a universe awaiting its creation,

an image of her sex, pinned in place
by piggy eyes in piggy perspiring faces.
Watching her writhe.

The gentle ungentle lights define
each fine electric hair, her passionless face
grained with the pain of primal grace,

and in the glittering heart of exposure
her smiling eyes are lacquered black as stars,
imploded, dark and dangerous as space.

Détente

The kettle siffles to a shrill
didactic whistle. Kitty is in her kitchen,
chopping parsley and logic.

Prague, Afghanistan, Poland:
the blade of meaning becoming blunt
from lying too long in the drawer of speech.

Dialectics, dialectics,
oregano, tarragon.
She read it all in *Newsweek*.

Fragrance of Chanel in the nape of her neck.
No doubt you're right, I say,
imagining my fingers in her hair.

One Damn Thing after another

The elementary logic of farewells
is a bore, you say, belittling yourself and over-
eager to confess to a hatred of tears. Your

father was found at the wheel of his taxi
this morning at three. The engine was ticking
over, the headlights were on. You describe how

you watched the rainwater filling into the
lilac, how the police light flashing
off the cobbles made you dizzy. Goodbye.

A nineteen-year-old GI. He'd thrown the
knife into the grass. His denim jacket
was in the back of the taxi, with his ID.

Aschaffenburg, you always used to say,
was a quiet town where nothing ever happened.
So mathematical! A castle

with twelve towers and fifty-two doors
and three hundred and sixty-five windows.
I've never checked it myself. But I take your point:

after a night like this you'll learn to hate
the cool exactness of sunlight calling forth
the daily confident enlightenment.

Your mother sent him a letter when
they were still engaged, breaking it off,
but somehow the letter fetched up in a sack

of mail for Asia, and sat in a boat
in the Suez Canal for years, really, for years,
till they opened it up again. By then

your parents had long been married, and you were eight
and learning the violin, and one day, a Tuesday,
the letter arrived, and your father never

felt safe in his love again. Imagine it: how
the daily hello of living disintegrates.
Goodbye goodbye goodbye goodbye goodbye.

I have a plane to make, but I'll listen
here on the windy platform, till my train comes in;
you'll tell me whatever histories you will,

until the hysteria gets the better of you. I
will write you a letter from the departure lounge
in Frankfurt. You ought to be with your mother.

**Programmatic Portrait: Carol Constance, Single, Twenty-Six,
Reading Saki in the London Underground**

Actually the meaning of life is
here in her handbag: a handkerchief
initialled white on white at the corner,

ideal for those long goodbyes. Or
else it is in her basket filled with bread
and celery sticks and honey and

a bottle of Sandeman's sherry. Or
it is here in the story she is reading:
she turns the page, wondering about

the stricken stag, the unseeing huntsman,
the hungry wolves, and Nicholas, the boy.
It is a story. Why feel so afraid?

She crosses her legs. Her feet
are size four. She can dance
more spirited than sperm or spirochaete.

This may be a poem of the low mimetic
but that doesn't mean I don't care for this stranger.
I could add that her hair is golden as

an oriole's head, but the image isn't one
a reader can respond to any longer,
and Edna Longley would write some more of her crap

about portentousness. Instead I write:
Carol has travelled quite enough
this eastbound Central stretch

from Holborn out to Redbridge and
her bedsit with its forty-watt reading light
in a turquoise shade above the bed.

It is a year or more since she went near
a dance-hall or a disco: fear
of the unforeseen chance that pinions a woman

against the dark alley wall keeps Carol at home.
She knows no one — no one she'd want to know
for life, with trust. And love. And need.

Her life *is* low mimetic: Liverpool Street,
Bethnal Green, Mile End, slow as an ageing nun
saying the rosary. The stations go

like beliefs relinquished, with brief haste which
suggests a quicker living, bitch
and dog, fever and drug, victim

screaming to victim in
the rituals of unironic sin:
it is all murder on the Central Line,

and in that peaceful panic scene
on a lumber-room screen
she sees how we live, caught between

killing and being killed.

Correspondence Course

In letters from Jakarta and Tangier,
in beautiful calligraphy, a hand
trained for the sweet secrets of the sealed word,
   how effortlessly she conferred
   a costly value on her *Dear* . . .
An artless art. A beauty barely bland.

She taught me nothing of herself. I read
of litmus summer sunsets in Bordeaux,
of visits to the Salzburg Festival —
   the strange, incommunicable
   innuendoes of the unsaid.
Something there always was I didn't know:

herself. She was defined by distance. In
her air there was a brighter oxygen,
such as surrounds a woman by Vermeer:
   a rare, translucent atmosphere.
   Hers was written fear, conducting
perfect friendships at the tip of her pen.

Fear of Flying

In hellfire tailcoat like
a Fortnum and Mason homunculus,
   the ringmaster gleefully points
like John the Baptist up at the trapeze:
      he knows the fantasies

   and secret angst of those
whose art is aerobiological,
   their fear of the act falling flat.
Out on the frail event's circumference
   the staggered audience

      stares: *snack! snack!* cracks his whip,
and, prompt as horses, the five acrobats
   tumble and skip into the ring.
Let's have a big hand! The judgement of Paris . . .
   A Tenniel Alice,

   a bland head-banded blonde
with dancing slippers on her tiny feet,
   is the first to fall: down, down, down.
Dinah missed her. The ringmaster snaps his
      whip, the spell collapses,

   and helpless in the net
the girl thrashes and snatches at the edge,
   bundles bravely under, catches
the mood of disillusion in the crowd,
   and crumples, bloody, bowed.

Harry Houdini

Expert in pseudo-suicide,
  past master at escaping from
the iron maiden of reality,
the punitive confinement of the womb,
cruel accouchement — Harry Houdini,
    Poe-faced prisoner of pride,

  tell us the meaning of the chains
   and manacles, the six deep feet
of premature burial in the earth.
What kind of metaphysical conceit
made you imagine purgatory worth
    the tortured anguish and pains

  of escape from greater hells? Did
   mother smother and stultify
and terrify you with love? Did father
muffle to a suffocated death? Why,
before you dared to breathe, did you rather
    take on the terrible pit

  and pendulum of fear? *The sound*
   of the ugly jugular throb
sobbing through my skull was all my joy. Death
paid danger money, and I took the job:
sarcophagi and coffins: the sweet breath
    of life six feet underground.

Department-store Dreamplay

. . . for underneath the shiny paint it was made of nothing but plaster!
Beatrix Potter, *The Tale of Two Bad Mice*

Dressed in dung-brown dungarees, two
    assistants are
destroying the cool impromptu
room. It is like a theatre:

but what action, we wonder, calls
    so callously
for the absence of all four walls?
Dismantling it impassively,

the two assistants do not seem
    to be aware
of the room's nakedness. Tom Thumb
moves as in a dream, exposure

the least of his worries. He strips
    pullover, shirt
and pants off men with plastic hips.
It doesn't even seem to hurt

when Tom Thumb amputates their arms.
    All of the men
have been unsexed; the women's charms
will never launch a ship again.

Their nudity invests the scene
    with true tragic
pathos (cathartic): a serene
sense of departmental logic.

Frugal Hunca Munca dashes
    away to store
the props (Coke cans, Cornflakes packets),
but presently returns with more,

to build a new illusion. In
    the changed display
the androgynes are sipping gin
and eating dreamplay canapés.

III

Laßt uns eine Reise tun! Laßt uns unter Zypressen
oder auch unter Palmen oder in den Orangenhainen
zu verbilligten Preisen Sonnenuntergänge sehen,
die nicht ihresgleichen haben! Laßt uns die
unbeantworteten Briefe an das Gestern vergessen!
Die Zeit tut Wunder.

Ingeborg Bachmann

At Aigues-Mortes

*I should like to restore to every subject its weight
and volume, and not only paint the appearance.*
Frédéric Bazille

This is the idea of a day,
this line where land and sky
defy the definition of the eye.

This is the flat
extremity
of extraordinary life:

the levelled end
of the uneven privilege of hills
and the gentle unbending

of rivers and vineyards.
This is elsewhere,
the perfect unending.

Squat-solid at the open-ended scape
the massive majesty of walls,
delineating immanence:

permanence of instinct
properly informing
impermanence of form.

The emblematic act
translates idea
into fact.

Thinking of Bazille, who stood
where I stand now, knowing
that all the strange extremity

of immanence could not atone
for art's apartness, nor restore
propriety to living's dislocations,

I realize we're all the same,
crusading to a holy land
of inviolability.

Psalm for Somoza, 1964

after Ernesto Cardenal

It is that twilight time when the faithful
assemble for the evening mass
and the church seems full of devils.

It is the time of darkness, the time
of shadows, the time of awareness.
My past thickens. *My sin is always with me.*

And while we recite the psalms, memory
thrusts its intrusive presence into my prayer
like the blare of a juke box or a radio.

Familiar films and nightmares, hotel room boredom,
dances and kisses and bars, endless journeys.
Forgotten faces. Mysterious evil.

Dead Somoza quits his mausoleum,
with Sihon, king of the Amorites,
and Og, king of Bashan.

The lights of the Copacabana
glitter under the jetty in the black
cloacal waters of Managua.

Meaningless conversation in the night,
stuck like a drunk in stupid repetition
like a scratched record.

Excitement at the roulette wheels!
Excitement at the juke box!
My sin is always with me.

Lights shine like stars in brothels and bars.
Caiaphas holds open house tonight,
and brightness explodes in Somoza's palace.

It is the time for councils of war to meet,
when smiling torturers
prowl the passageways of filthy prisons,

and spies and the secret police
come into their own. Thieves and adulterers
lurk in dark back alleys and cul-de-sacs,

and corpses are pushed into cupboards.
A body splashes into the water.
It is the time for the dying to die.

It is the time for the agony in the garden,
the time for the final temptation.
The first birds are confident of the sun,

but here it is still the time of darkness
when the church is as cold as the devil's abode,
and we go on reciting psalms to the night.

Brunei

Down Jalan Sultan the Datsuns burn,
exulting, declaiming:
we shall inherit the earth.

Querulous, squalling, squealing like kids at the dodgems:
the neurasthenic staccatissimo
of acquisition in action.

When we arrived, and entered the port, and anchored,
the holy body of brightness, the beautiful fire,
burned like the tongues of deity high in the dark.

Stitching in and out the spindle stilts,
Suzuki outboard motors split
the water village stillness, taking

Moslem girls in white and blue to school.
Women are hanging the washing out,
and up the rickety walkway races

Brunei's young executive,
pin-striped trousers, attaché case, and late,
making the frail stilettos creak and sway.

The morning of the following day, the ninth of July,
the king of the island sent a magnificent prau
with workings in gold at bow and stern

and banners of blue and white and peacock feathers.
Their chiefs presented us with a painted jar
filled with betel and areca, a fruit,

two cages full of fowls, and sugarcane, and goats,
and jars of spirit, called arak. The spirit of these people
is clear as water, and very strong.

The hovels are balanced on their stalks
precarious as dandelion clocks.
The river slubbers, lapping at

the slobby mudflats, slopping at
rotting rats and bottles, bamboo poles,
cans and tyres and crappy scum.

The river drivels dirty yellow.
The swimming children love it.
We were taken on elephant-back to visit the king,

and seven bearers went ahead with gifts:
velvet robes and velvet-covered chairs,
a gilded writing-case, and silvered shoes.

The king of Spain, their king declared,
shall be my friend.
Three hundred naked guards with rapiers

smiled with a single smile
that slit along the sides of the great hall
like a slash from a blade.

Leaving Jakarta

The airport superflux:
a transport plane's pregnant sag,
bellied like a water buffalo;

a turbo-prop revving up,
blades chopping round
like tassels on a topless dancer's tits;

the fetid underworld of heat,
the buzzing shimmering
that hammers on the tarmac of the heart.

Snapping the paper open like a napkin:
newsprint greys my thumbs, like
a priest's Ash Wednesday smudge.

Rice Terraces in Java

Tiered like rococo steps
they ravel round the hills,
contour lines on a map.

The sky is television grey,
quicksilvers in the water's glass,
pricked with pins of lucent green.

In one field a man is stooping, planting,
perfectly rounded like a croquet hoop.
A second is sitting amid the cabbages

where red and yellow canna splash
Spanish flags across the green
and fuchsia and pink periwinkle grow.

Evening at Imogiri

The bullock carts are pulling back along
the homeward road, below the hillside where
the spirits of the Javan kings confer
knowledge of heaven on the empty air.

The cool of evening light, the cool of time
received and seen: the meanings of the day
fading, changing. Cold perceptions of night
a single cigarette away.

At kitchens by the wayside women sit,
shrivelled into a silence and a mask,
like matchlit faces in a cinema.
And frangipani falling in the dusk.

The Cemetery at Trunyan

Bali

At the dark charnel showground they
have wrapped her naked in newspaper.
She died two days ago.

From the village they rowed her here
to the passionless shade, and laid her out
on the bare earth. Above her they stood

a wicker trellis like criss-crossed beanpoles,
to keep off animals.
When tourists come in boats

to see the corpses and old anonymous bones,
they pass a hat round. Collecting
dead money for the living.

Cockfight

Bali

Leaving their wives behind
to cook and fetch water and mind
the children, the diligent men
assemble and smile and submit
to the sense of event, expecting pain,
a ritual sense of death and debt:

now there is nothing more
but palm wine, betting, and honour
that fastens a bright blade of steel
to the foot of a fowl, nothing
other than killing, a bloody bundle
of feathers, nothing: now. Strutting

cock-of-the-walk and proud
the owners go about the crowd
to show their killers off; the cocks
blink with a bland, unflinching stare,
that scathing gaze of the heterodox
that cancels an aggressive air

and neuters pomp . . . yet still
they clinch firm for the coming kill
when presently they're set to face.
The bellow of the betting dies.
The birds circle, setting a civil pace,
filled with a fixed will, in their eyes

a cunning common sense,
a calm, vindictive innocence
that isn't instinct. Then a rush,
a flash of the spur, a sparring
and flapping, a battering rage, a slash,
and one cock drags beyond caring

away into cover,
pulsing blood: and the fight's over
as suddenly as it began.
Death and debts are settled, and here
comes the next cock-stepping parading man,
martially bargaining with fear.

Helicopter

We are leaving them behind, the children,
who played in the dust for butterflies pinned on card,
    for buttons or cartridge cases:
leaving, leaving them all, for faraway places
    with faraway names. Overhead
  a chopper, cropping our last contrition

  as easily as a boy with a stick
dispatches thistle-heads, riots a slow, roaring
    descent to the embassy roof:
and one arrival rifles our silence of love,
    of the truths we had been shoring
  against our future. Now we are all sick.

  We are leaving, leaving. Impolitic
to stay. Imprudent. Impossible. And the men
    who biked the long hot dusty roads
to bring us the news, and carried our chosen loads
    out of the last hotels, have gone,
  knowing we're going. Now we are all sick.

  We are sick in strange ways, and with a pain
we thought belonged in other lives; and we climb high
    from the scene of our crimes, needing
escape from the heat, the helplessness, the bleeding,
    battering to an angry sky
  where thunder breeds, bringing releasing rain.

Ballad of the Legionnaire

after Helga M. Novak

I've nothing to eat for you today
said mother   I'm already on my way
said her son   and took the legion's pay

first they sent him to Algiers
bullets tattered both his ears

then Korea for a year
the sheer hell of it greyed his hair

in Madagascar in the sand
he found he lacked his left hand

he lost the sight of an eye in Chad
they said: we'll buy you a glass one, lad

so then he returned to Algeria
which cost him a piece of his lower jaw

in the jungle of Tahiti
they shot away his virility

and then at length in Dien Bien Phu
he lost a foot along with its shoe

in Djibouti in a fever he tossed
tormented by the limbs he'd lost

in the Congo he played the firebrand
and paid for it with his other hand

age twenty-eight he went home once more
his mother said   what son of a whore
is this?   and showed him out the door

A Pill-box near Stavanger

I

Slit-eyed like a Teuton helmet
the pill-box faces
the savage waves,

atop a crop
of craggy rock
and jagged wire:

brave as propagated faith,
stern as Norway's forehead
set to the northern sea —

keeping its solitary watch,
blind as the present tense,
passive, angry, forgotten.

Falkenhorst used a Baedeker to plan
the conquest of Norway. Now in my hand
I hold a weathered Baedeker and read

the dank breathing of weed,
the dark scud of cloud,
plotting the height

of history measured against a man.
A man like myself.
How small I am.

II

Here in this blackrock eye of water I found
a woman's sandal, a white champagne-glass sandal
with delicate straps and a high stem,

and now, straining to stand, rammed
by the roar of the ugly wind, I think of a woman
walking barefoot down to the rabid sea:

razor grass grazes her naked legs
with hieroglyphs of thin red,
like bloodied barbed wire;

her dress
is pressed against her body by the wind;
her hair is tangled in Atlantic strands —

an Aphrodite of perversity,
returning to the mania
of grey marine and white naked spray,

walking down to the cruel sea where the wire
rusts to the rock and the waves rush in from the dark
and banging anger of Stavanger's hungry salt,

the water language of anguish and war.

On Location

for Peter and Odile Wagner

This superannuated Bavarian town
   of crumbling baroque and flaking façades
is the perfect backdrop for these shameful charades.
   It is a dull place which neither renown
nor notoriety has ever disgraced, so
   it is only fitting that this film crew
should choose to engender their legend of a Jew,
   his Aryan wife, and the Gestapo
here on this unhistoric square (for, after all,
   the innocent present is the fittest
set on which to play actions of the guilty past,
   since there we see the full ironical
force of historical fact). Thus the director
   sits in his canvas chair smoking cigars,
snapping Hollywood commandments at timid stars,
   his belly in his lap, his green visor
pushed back into his straight black hair. Incessantly
   the make-up girl paints, the clapperboard snaps,
and cameras capture the frail, final (perhaps)
   fitness of inevitability,
filming reality into fiction, fiction
   into reality: who can tell which?
With luck this movie will make its producer rich,
   will even be seen on television
in Israel and the States, Japan and Germany.
   Tourists who visit this town in future
will tell each other that was Aaron's house, and there
   was where he said goodbye to Rosemary.

Nuremberg

Pegnitz in Flammen

Soldiers punting
a pontoon raft
along the river: pink bunting,
and Bengal lighting burning fore and aft.

This is a part
of the new deal
we have a title to: the art
of illusion illuminates the real,

and fireworks spell
anemones
of brightness black and red as hell.
We can no more enlarge their obsequies.

JUN 5 1986

DATE DUE